IMAGES
*of America*

# THE
# TUSKEGEE
# AIRMEN

IMAGES
*of America*

# THE
# TUSKEGEE
# AIRMEN

Lynn M. Homan and Thomas Reilly

ARCADIA

Published by Arcadia Publishing,
an imprint of Tempus Publishing, Inc.
2 Cumberland Street
Charleston, SC 29401

Printed in Great Britain.

Library of Congress Catalog Card Number: 98-88301

For all general information contact Arcadia Publishing at:
Telephone 843-853-2070
Fax 843-853-0044
E-Mail arcadia@charleston.net

For customer service and orders:
Toll-Free 1-888-313-BOOK

Visit us on the internet at http://www.arcadiaimages.com

# CONTENTS

# ACKNOWLEDGMENTS

The genesis of this book was a museum exhibition on the Tuskegee Airmen that we curated and produced in 1996. As part of our research and preparation, we traveled throughout the United States interviewing several dozen Tuskegee Airmen and their families. They graciously gave of their time and very generously shared their remembrances, photographs, and three-dimensional artifacts.

We are indebted to Lee A. Archer, Charles P. Bailey, LeRoy A. Battle, Henry C.L. Bohler, Eugene Clark, Woodrow W. Crockett, Arque B. Dickerson, Alvin J. Downing, Bunny G. Downing, Roscoe Draper, Jean R. Esquerre, Edwina W. Ford, Harry E. Ford, Charles R. Foxx, Charles A. Hill, Mary M. Hill, James A. Hurd, Theopolis W. Johnson, Elmer D. Jones, Haldane King, Julius Ligon, Hiram E. Mann, Kathadaza Mann, Charles E. McGee, Frankie C. Minnis, Peggy Peterman, Louis R. Purnell, Maury M. Reid, Sherman Rose, Raymond F. Sanderlin, Fenton B. Sands, Robert Saunders, Harry A. Sheppard, Harry T. Stewart, John J. Suggs, Andrew D. Turner Jr., Spann Watson, Yenwith K. Whitney, Donald A. Williams, James E. Wright, Nasby Wynn, and many others. Directly involved with the Tuskegee Experience, each took the time to help us understand, as best we could, what it was like to be an African-American in the 1940s. Without the assistance of Tess Spooner and Hank Sanford, both of Tuskegee Airmen, Inc., many of our contacts would not have been made possible. Dr. Florence T. Parrish-St. John and William F. Holton offered many interesting and valuable insights into the Tuskegee Experience.

Brian Nicklas of the Smithsonian Institution's National Air and Space Museum was especially helpful in assisting us with the acquisition of photographs of pioneer African-American aviators, as well as those who served in World War II, Korea, and Vietnam. Photographs from the National Aeronautics and Space Administration are of paramount importance in illustrating the quantum leap that has been made since the segregationist Jim Crow era. Donnie Cochran, the first African-American to fly with the Navy's Blue Angels demonstration team, also provided a photograph. As always, Kelly, Bruce, and the staff at Zebra Color Photo Lab worked their magic to copy 50-year-old photographs to be better than the originals.

We are especially grateful to Hiram and Kathadaza Mann and Louis Purnell for their constant support and encouragement.

# INTRODUCTION

Long before most Americans believed that blacks could fly, African-American men and women were contributing to the field of aviation. Some achieved fame; hundreds of unheralded others did their best to "fill the air with black wings." Eugene Jacques Bullard, unable to become a pilot in the United States Army in World War I, became a pilot in the French Air Force and the first African-American to fly a military airplane. Bessie Coleman became the first African-American to be licensed to fly when she received her Fédération Aéronautique Internationale certificate in June 1921.

The team of Dr. Albert E. Forsythe and C. Alfred "Chief" Anderson exposed hundreds of thousands of Americans to the prospect of black aviators with their well-publicized long-distance flights in 1933 and 1934. During the 1940s, Cornelius R. Coffey and Willa Brown promoted an all-black Air Derby, started the first flight school owned and operated by African-Americans, and were instrumental in the creation of the National Airmen's Association of America. Brown was the first black woman to serve in the Civil Air Patrol.

Following World War I, several studies were made regarding the role of African-Americans in the military. The studies were exercises to prove that blacks were inferior to whites and were suited only for menial positions. The War Department held the position that, "The colored man had not been attracted to flying in the same way or to the extent of the white man." African-Americans felt a strong patriotic need to serve in their country's military services, however, and they fought to do so.

Many black newspapers waged a gallant and steady editorial battle to open the military to African-Americans. In mid-January 1941, Yancey Williams, a black Howard University student, filed a lawsuit over the rejection of his application as a flying cadet. On January 16, 1941, the War Department relented, announcing that African-Americans would be allowed to become Air Corps pilots. An all-black unit, the 99th Pursuit Squadron, would be activated. The press conference announcing the formation of the 99th stated that 35 black candidates would be chosen from the Civilian Pilot Training Program.

When the Army Air Corps opened to African-Americans, Tuskegee, Alabama, a stronghold of racial segregation, intolerance, and lawlessness against blacks, was selected as the training site. The 99th Pursuit Squadron (later re-designated as the 99th Fighter Squadron) would consist of 33 to 35 pilots and approximately 300 ground crew members. The first officers would be white; as African-American officers were trained, they would take command of the squadron. Fifteen weeks of primary training, which included ground school, meteorology, and principals of flight, would take place at Tuskegee Institute. Secondary training would occur at Tuskegee Army Air Field, which was still to be built.

The first group of African-Americans entered the pilot training program in July 1941. Class 42-C, the first class, consisted of only 13 men. The base was segregated and controlled by white officers. Conditions were not good. The situation off base was worse. On March 7, 1942, Lemuel R. Custis, Charles DeBow, Mac Ross, George Spencer Roberts, and Captain Benjamin O. Davis Jr. graduated from the program. Eight men had "washed out" (been eliminated).

By mid-1942, Tuskegee Army Air Field was home to approximately 217 officers and 3,000 enlisted men. Colonel Frederick von Kimble, the base commander, enforced a strict segregation policy. "Colored" and "white" signs were posted on all facilities. Under von Kimble's successor, Colonel Noel F. Parrish, the segregation of the base was reduced.

Demand for pilot training was great. Since Tuskegee was the only training facility for African-American pilots, a quota of 200 men per year was established. Hundreds applied for the rare openings; many ended up on a long waiting list. More were drafted into the army and never received their chance to fly. At the same time, the War Department desperately needed and advertised for pilots. The demand, however, was for white pilots, not black. Young African-American men waited, many in vain.

Life at Tuskegee Army Air Field had many aspects. Military training, flight instruction, and academic studies were difficult and filled most of the hours. Accommodations in the barracks provided few amenities. Even the most dedicated cadets needed some relaxation, however. Strict segregation and an unwelcome atmosphere in surrounding communities made visits into town less than pleasant. Most social and recreational activities took place at the base. Wives, mothers, and sweethearts filled an important role in the lives of the cadets. All shared the triumphs and rejoiced in the accomplishments. Each suffered the sorrows and endured the slights and humiliations. Graduation ceremonies were frequently accompanied by weddings.

Over 10,000 African-American men and women served as support personnel. They were crew chiefs, flight chiefs, technical inspectors, armorers, dispatchers, parachute repairmen, and shop men including welders, machinists, propeller experts, painters, and electricians. While these troops on the ground have received little credit, without them the pilots could not have functioned. The planes would have been unable to fly.

While some people kept the planes in the air, others performed the vital functions necessary to the running of any large organization. Clerical workers handled the paperwork of payrolls, promotions, and duty assignments. Draftsmen provided statistics, as well as blueprints for projects to be built by construction workers. Doctors, dentists, and nurses saw to the medical care of the troops. Musicians entertained at various military functions, war bond rallies, and recreational performances. Motor pool drivers and mechanics, supply clerks, cooks, photographers, etc. handled the thousands of jobs of daily army life.

The importance of women to the success of the Tuskegee Experience has received little attention. The emotional support, motivation, and encouragement provided by mothers, sweethearts, and wives was extremely important. On the field itself, African-American women were instrumental in various aspects of training. Some women served as aircraft mechanics on the flight line and as parachute riggers. Cecilia Dixon of Columbia, South Carolina, served as an aircraft dispatcher at Tuskegee. Other women worked in the fabric repair department and as clerks in the quartermaster and signal corps.

The ratio of support personnel to pilots for the first squadron was approximately 14 to 1. As more pilots were trained, the ratio diminished to 10 to 1. Enlisted men and women performed work that was vital to the success of the fliers. Most pilots realized this, and readily acknowledged the value of the support personnel.

Approximately 65 classes of pilots graduated at Tuskegee Army Air Field. Following the formation of the 99th, pilots subsequently filled the ranks of three more fighter squadrons—the 100th, the 301st, and the 302nd. Collectively these three squadrons formed the 332nd Fighter Group. Later, joined by the 99th Fighter Squadron, they were the only fighter group made up of four squadrons. Shortly after the last class graduated in June 1946, the base closed. Under the harsh restrictions of segregation, the African-American cadets both trained and served together. This forced isolation forged an unbreakable bond between the participants in the Tuskegee Experience.

On April 2, 1943, the pilots and crews of the 99th Fighter Squadron finally left Tuskegee Army Air Field, headed for Europe. Four hundred members of the 99th along with 3,500 white troops steamed out of a Brooklyn, New York, port aboard the SS *Mariposa* destined for North Africa. In combat, the 99th's mission was to escort bombers and ship convoys and perform low-level strafing and dive-bombing of targets. On the morning of June 9, 1943, the 99th experienced combat for the first time, escorting 12 bombers on a mission to Pantelleria, Italy. January 27, 1944, was one of the most successful days of the European campaign for the 99th. On a routine morning flight, the pilots spotted a group of German fighters attacking Allied ships. Before the smoke of cannon fire had cleared, six enemy planes had been shot down.

The record of the African-American fighter pilots was magnificent. Four hundred and fifty pilots flew more than 1,500 missions. They destroyed 111 enemy airplanes in the air and another 150 on the ground in strafing missions. One destroyer escort and 57 locomotives were also put out of commission.

The all-black 477th Bombardment Group (Medium) was activated in May 1943, at Selfridge Field, Michigan. The leaders of the Air Corps and the War Department had no interest in African-American pilots commanding bombers. The 477th Bombardment Group was formed because of an undiminished pressure from black leaders, newspapers, unions, and civic groups. The men of the 477th paid dearly for the privilege of breaking down yet another military barrier to African-Americans. From the time their training began at Tuskegee, the men of the 477th experienced some of the most bitter racism of any of the black units ever formed. Constantly confronted with racism, segregation, and frustration as they attempted to train, the 477th Bombardment Group was transferred from base to base in an effort to destroy morale.

Originally commanded by Colonel Robert R. Selway, a white officer known for his racist sentiments, the group was never sent overseas. Their losses came not at the hands of the enemy, but from their own countrymen. After the war in Europe ended, Colonel Benjamin O. Davis Jr. assumed command of the 477th Composite Group on July 1, 1945. The Composite Group consisted of both bomber and fighter aircraft.

By the end of the war, almost 1,000 young African-Americans had graduated from the pilot training program at Tuskegee Army Air Field. Of these, 450 pilots served overseas. Nearly 900 decorations were awarded to these men. The record of the all-black Army Air Corps units during World War II proved that African-American pilots were not only able to learn to fly sophisticated airplanes, but were more than capable of performing admirably in combat. Equally important, the accomplishments of these men were unmistakable in the magnitude of social change they helped to create.

President Harry Truman's order in 1948 to desegregate the military was brought about in part by the success of the black fliers and the Tuskegee Experience. The program developed hundreds of fine military officers and leaders among the black ranks who worked to insure that African-Americans had a future in the newly integrated military service of the United States. Pride in the black Army Air Corps members led to a tremendous boost in the self-esteem of all African-American men and women.

When North Korean troops attacked northwest of Seoul, South Korea, on June 25, 1950, American forces entered the conflict as part of a United Nations "police action" to force North Korean troops back beyond the 38th parallel. As combat units took casualties, openings were filled with replacements of both races. For the first time in American military history, African-Americans were received equally as American soldiers and airmen. Assignments were given on the basis of qualifications, not color.

Many of the men who had trained at Tuskegee Army Air Field during World War II saw action in Korea. Twenty-one black pilots from the 99th Fighter Squadron and the 332nd Fighter Group served in the Korean Conflict, as did hundreds of African-American enlisted men and women.

African-Americans first entered the United States Air Force Academy in the class of 1963. With America's involvement in Vietnam escalating, millions of young men and women, black and white, would soon be called to duty in yet another war. If Korea was the initial means of military integration, Vietnam provided near-equality of opportunity in the air and on the battlefields of Southeast Asia.

America's first manned space flight took place on May 5, 1961. Twenty-two years later, Guion S. Bluford became the first African-American to fly in space. As with the fighter and bomber squadrons of World War II, the efforts of many people are required to keep America's space program in operation. Approximately 1,000 technical, scientific, and engineering support personnel are needed to support each NASA astronaut. Many of these men and women are African-Americans.

The men and women of the Tuskegee Experience opened doors for future aviators. Guion Bluford, Frederick Gregory, Bernard Harris, Winston Scott, Robert Curbeam, Ronald McNair, Mae Jemison, and the many other African-American members of America's space program have gone beyond the boundaries to reach for the stars.

# One

# AFRICAN-AMERICAN AVIATION PIONEERS

Many Americans believed that African-Americans possessed neither the mental nor physical abilities necessary to fly airplanes. As the United States began to consider its possible involvement in the European war, military leaders began to plan for the training of pilots and construction of airplanes. Except in the most menial of capacities, blacks were not intended to be part of those plans. Patriotic African-Americans, black newspapers and labor organizations, and the NAACP intended otherwise, however. A bold gesture on the part of First Lady Eleanor Roosevelt furthered their cause. In 1940, C. Alfred Anderson, known to all as "Chief," took Mrs. Roosevelt for a flight above Alabama. Mrs. Roosevelt's report of her experience to President Franklin D. Roosevelt hastened the formation of the Tuskegee program. (C. Alfred Anderson via National Air and Space Museum, Smithsonian Institution, SI Neg. No. 90-7010.)

While the African-American fliers who became known as the Tuskegee Airmen were the first blacks to fly in the American military, African-Americans had been part of aviation almost from the beginning. These aviation pioneers had been confronted with the same biases and stereotypes as those faced by the Tuskegee Airmen. During World War I, Eugene Jacques Bullard served as a military pilot. Unable to find anyone to teach him to fly in America, Bullard, born in 1894 in Columbus, Georgia, traveled to France. There he became a pursuit pilot with the famed French Lafayette Flying Corps. Called the "Black Swallow of Death," Eugene Jacques Bullard was honored for his service with the French Legion of Honor, the Croix de Guerre, and several other awards. (National Air and Space Museum, Smithsonian Institution, SI Neg. No. 91-6283.)

Bessie Coleman, America's first licensed black pilot, promoted aviation for African-Americans throughout the United States during the 1920s. Unable to find anyone to teach her to fly in the United States, she eventually trained in France at the Ecole d' Aviation Des Fréres Caudron at Le Crotoy. It was in an old military-surplus open-cockpit Curtiss Jenny that Bessie Coleman lost her life on April 30, 1926, in Jacksonville, Florida. (National Air and Space Museum, Smithsonian Institution, SI Neg. No. 97-16153.)

James H. Banning and Thomas C. Allen, the "Flying Hoboes," were the first African-American aviators to make a transcontinental flight. On September 18, 1932, Banning and Allen left Los Angeles headed for New York with only $25 in their pockets. Twenty-one days later, they landed their eight-year-old Eagle Rock biplane at New York's Roosevelt Field. Their actual flying time had been 41 hours and 27 minutes. (Thomas C. Allen via National Air and Space Museum, Smithsonian Institution.)

J. Herman Banning
Pilot

Thomas C. Allen.
Mec.

FIRST TRANS-CONTINENTAL FLIGHT

Janet Bragg purchased the first airplane for John Robinson's Chicago-based Challenger Air Pilots Association in the 1930s. The Challenger Air Pilots Association was one of the groups which encouraged African-Americans to become involved in aviation. Bragg, a registered nurse, was a member of the Chicago Girls Flying Club. (Harold Hurd via National Air and Space Museum, Smithsonian Institution, SI Neg. No. 91-15485.)

Many hours of flying time had to be recorded before a cadet could earn his wings. C. Alfred "Chief" Anderson came to Tuskegee from the Civilian Pilot Training Program at Howard University. The group commander of the civilian flight instructors at Tuskegee, Anderson taught thousands of young African-Americans to fly during the course of his career. (Private Collection.)

Under the stewardship of Walter White, the National Association for the Advancement of Colored People waged a constant and vocal battle against the exclusionary policies of the United States War Department. White's goal was to convince the War Department to open the United States Army Air Corps to African-Americans. (NAACP Library.)

William H. Hastie, dean of the Howard University Law School and a graduate of Harvard University Law School, served for several years as a civilian advisor to Secretary of War Henry L. Stimson. When the War Department announced its decision to allow African-Americans to join the Air Corps, Hastie praised the change in policy. At the same time, he rejected the idea of continued segregation within the military. (NAACP Library.)

Although the admission requirements of the Army Air Corps made no mention of race, the applications of African-Americans were always rejected. In early January 1941, Yancey Williams, a graduate of Howard University, filed suit against the War Department for admittance to the Army Air Corps. Only days later, the War Department announced formation of an all-black fighter squadron. Eventually accepted into the flight program, Williams (back row, fourth from left) graduated on December 28, 1944, as a member of Class 44-K. Although his case never went to court, the potential threat of legal action is considered one of the reasons for the reversal of the War Department's "whites-only" policy. (Private Collection.)

## *Two*

# THE BEST TRAINING
# IN THE WORLD

The Army Air Corps promised "the best training in the world" to those men accepted for flight training. On July 19, 1941, Major General Walter R. Weaver, commander of the Southeast Training Center, stood in front of a monument to Booker T. Washington and addressed 13 men who hoped to be the first African-American Air Corps pilots. At the inauguration of the training program, he said, "The eyes of your country and the eyes of your people are upon you. You cannot be inoculated with the ability to fly. The life of a flying student is no bed of roses." Major James A. Ellison, the first commander of Tuskegee Army Air Field, returned the salute of Air Corps Cadet Mac Ross. By the end of the training, all but five members of Class 42-C had "washed out" (been eliminated). Benjamin O. Davis Jr., Mac Ross, Lemuel R. Custis, Charles DeBow, and George S. Roberts were the first graduates of the Tuskegee flying program. (United States Air Force.)

Civilian flight instructor Linkwood Williams played an important role at Tuskegee Army Air Field. During the primary course of training at Tuskegee, civilian flight instructors often gave young men their first introduction to flight. Others had received their beginning instruction in the Civilian Pilot Training Program that had been established in 1939. Only after cadets entered the later phases of the flight training program were their instructors white Air Corps officers. (Private Collection.)

The importance of civilian flight instructors at Tuskegee has long been unrecognized. Many of the instructors came from the Civilian Pilot Training Programs at African-American educational institutions such as Tuskegee, Howard, and Hampton, or the private companies headed by Cornelius Coffey and Willa Brown in Chicago. (Private Collection.)

The elimination or "wash-out" rate of black flying cadets at Tuskegee was higher than that of white cadets at other bases. A quota system mandated by the Air Corps was responsible for the elimination of many fine black pilots from the flight program. Calvin R. Harris washed out of flight training and became one of the cadre of civilian flight instructors who taught hundreds of black cadets to fly. (Private Collection.)

A pair of civilian flight instructors stood in front of a North American AT-6 trainer. Before the flight cadets graduated from flight training and transitioned into pursuit aircraft such as the P-39, P-40, and P-47, the AT-6 was the most sophisticated airplane they had flown. With its 650-horsepower engine and retractable landing gear, the AT-6 was used to practice combat maneuvers. (Private Collection.)

Throughout the course of flight training at Tuskegee Institute and Tuskegee Army Air Field, several different flying fields were used. Kennedy Field, Moton Field, and the military field at the air base each offered different phases of training. The flight line at Tuskegee Institute's Moton Field constantly hummed with activity. At any given time, there were at least one hundred airplanes of many different types here. (Private Collection.)

Mechanics of the 66th Army Air Forces Flying Training Detachment ensured that the airplanes used by the aviation cadets at Tuskegee Institute's Moton Field were in tip-top shape. The maintenance and repair of the antiquated aircraft was a full-time job. Many of the novice fliers owed their lives to the careful workmanship of the mechanics. (Private Collection.)

The position of tower operator at Moton Field was held by Mrs. Young. The importance of women in the Tuskegee Experience cannot be underestimated. At Tuskegee, African-American women filled many traditional and non-traditional occupations such as mechanics, parachute riggers, clerks, and librarians. (Private Collection.)

With air fields at Tuskegee Institute and Tuskegee Army Air Field and hundreds of airplanes on the ground and in the air, the air field tower was one of the busiest facilities. Each day, several hundred takeoffs and landings occurred. It was the responsibility of the tower operator to ensure a smooth and safe flow of aerial traffic. (Private Collection.)

Reveille officially began the day, although the cadets' sleep was frequently disrupted by upperclassmen. Various forms of hazing included recitation of "dodo" verses. "Sir: The cow, she walks, she talks, she's full of chalk. The lacteal fluid extracted from the female of the bovine species is highly prolific to the nth degree . . ." was just one example. (Private Collection.)

The difficulties of flying military aircraft required pilots to be in top physical condition. An extensive routine of calisthenics was part of the training program each day. Cadets who barely made the minimum weight requirement at their entrance physical exams quickly gained new muscles during the rigorous training. (Private Collection.)

Cadets at Tuskegee Army Air Field trained on several types of aircraft, including BT-13s, PT-17s, AT-6s, and P-40s. The airplanes varied in sophistication, from antique biplanes to high-speed pursuit aircraft. Each type of aircraft had its own idiosyncrasies. Airmen had to master each type of airplane before moving on to the next level of training. (United States Air Force.)

Aviation cadet Lloyd Scott Hathcock, a member of the Class of 43-K-SE, received congratulations from Colonel Frederick von Kimble for his skill in handling a primary training plane. Colonel von Kimble, an avowed segregationist, replaced Major James Ellison to become Tuskegee's second commander. (United States Air Force.)

At the beginning of the flight training program at Tuskegee Army Air Field, all flight cadets were required to have a four-year college education. As the program evolved, the cadets were accepted with only a high school education. In order to better prepare the trainees, they were first assigned to the 2211th Air Base Unit as part of the College Training Detachment. Over a period of several months, the cadets were exposed to intensive academic training. (Private Collection.)

Aviation cadets assigned to the College Training Detachment at Tuskegee Institute lived on campus and were transported to nearby flying fields for flight training. The pressure on these cadets was tremendous. A 12- to 15-hour day not only included rigorous academic studies, but also flight training and ground school classes. (Private Collection.)

Four members of Class 44-F were photographed during training at Tuskegee Army Air Field. Hugh White, Charles Hill, Lincoln Hudson, and Carl Ellis all graduated as single-engine pilots in June 1944. Cadets came from all parts of the United States. These four, along with many of their classmates, came from the Midwest, long a hub of African-American aviation. (Private Collection.)

Cadets from Class 44-F lined up in formation prior to ground school class, where they studied principles of flight, map reading, and meteorology. Upon graduation, 15 men received commissions as second lieutenants and another 11 became flight officers. Several of these men were later captured or killed during combat in Europe. (Private Collection.)

Seven of the single-engine pilots who had just graduated in Class 44-F at Tuskegee Army Air Field proudly posed for a photograph. The next destination for pilots Richard Armistead, Robert Lawrence, Harry Stewart, Frank Wright, Yenwith Whitney, Wyrain Schell, and George Lynch was combat readiness training at Walterboro Army Air Field in Walterboro, South Carolina. Following their instruction at Walterboro, ten days leave allowed the men to visit families across the nation. They then embarked for Italy to serve as replacement pilots for the combat-weary veterans of the 332nd Fighter Group. (Private Collection.)

Colonel Noel F. Parrish directed the training program at Tuskegee, becoming commander in February 1943. A leader with a sincere interest in making the flying program at Tuskegee successful and a belief in the racial equality of his men, Parrish was responsible for the removal of the "colored" and "white" signs on the base. As a pilot who had almost washed out during his own training program because of a conflict with an instructor, Parrish was determined that the cadets under his command would be treated as fairly as possible. His career was frequently in jeopardy as he worked within a segregated Air Corps for the success of a program which many of the top military leaders wanted to fail. Many of the Tuskegee Airmen believe that Parrish had an important role in the success of the program. (Noel F. Parrish via National Air and Space Museum, Smithsonian Institution.)

The men still needed to eat, even while away from the dining hall. Field kitchens provided meals to the men while on bivouac. After a long day of forced marches through woods and swamps while carrying 50-pound packs of equipment, cadets welcomed a hot meal almost as much as a hot shower and a soft bed. (Private Collection.)

Training at Tuskegee was more than just learning to fly airplanes. Marches and maneuvers in the field were all part of the preparation for combat. Living in tents was good practice for the African-American airmen. Advanced gunnery and bombing training required the 99th Fighter Squadron to fly to Dale Mabry Field, in Tallahassee, Florida. Forbidden to sleep in the barracks because of segregation, they were forced to sleep outdoors in pup tents. (Private Collection.)

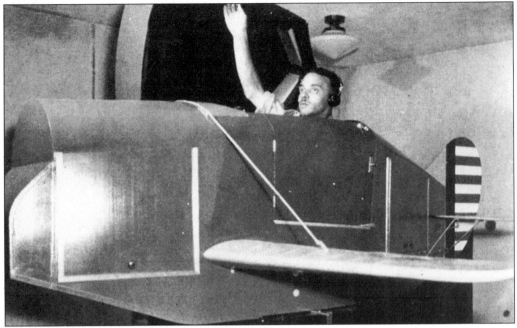

Hours were spent learning flight maneuvers in a Link Trainer. Little more than a rudimentary plywood box, the Link Trainer was often the first introduction to aviation for many would-be pilots. Neither aircraft nor people were expendable. These training sessions allowed beginning pilots to practice flying while still on the ground. (Private Collection.)

Taught by a sergeant trained at Chanute Army Air Field, a class on the intricacies of a Hamilton Standard variable-pitch propeller was part of the training program for cadets at Tuskegee Army Air Field. The men were expected to understand the mechanical aspects of the aircraft they were learning to fly. (Private Collection.)

To ensure safe flying and operational efficiency, aviation cadets underwent intensive training. Each day, the novice pilots spent several hours studying their manuals before actual flying. Lift, thrust, and the Bernoulli effect, alien concepts prior to their arriving at Tuskegee, became as familiar to the cadets as the names of their loved ones at home. (Private Collection.)

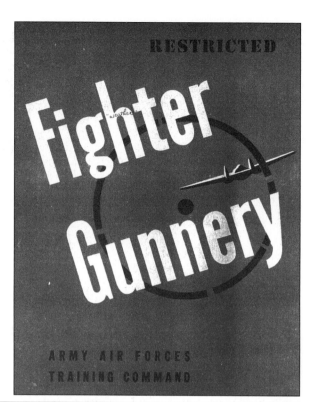

RESTRICTED

# Fighter Gunnery

ARMY AIR FORCES
TRAINING COMMAND

STUDY CARD—STUDENT'S COPY     Major _____

STUDY CARD—STUDENT'S COPY     Major _____     Ao

Use Ink
Course  43-C-11
Class  3ro C.T.D.

XXXXXXXXXXXXXXX

Pre Flight Training

Minor _____

Student ____Reid  maury  McKinley  JR.____
Last Name        First Name        Middle Name

| SUBJECT | ~KS. SUB. NO. | CR. HRS. | M. | T. | W. | TH. | F. | S. | BUILDING AND ROOM | INSTRUCTOR |
|---|---|---|---|---|---|---|---|---|---|---|
| Mil. C+C. | 15-16 | | 7 | 7 | 7 | 7 | 7 | | H.S. 103 | 210 |
| Hyg. & Sanit. | 17-18 | | 7 | 7 | 7 | 7 | 7 | | H.S. 103 | |
| Phys. Lec. | 19-30 | | 7 | 7 | 7 | 7 | 7 | | A. H. 103 | F.C. miller |
| Math. | 15-30 | | 8 | 8 | 8 | 8 | 8 | | H.S. 107 | J.F. Fuller |
| Mek. Aid. | 15-18 | | 9 | 9 | 9 | 9 | 9 | | H.S. 107 | W. J. Love |
| History | 19-30 | | 9 | 9 | 9 | 9 | 9 | | H.S. 114 | H. J. Romm |
| Phys. Lab. | 19-30 | | 10 | 10 | 10 | 10 | 10 | | A. H. 101 | W. mc Ruge |
| Phys. Lab. | 19-70 | | 11 | 11 | 11 | 11 | 11 | | A. H. 101 | "MS Cormick-" |
| Phys. Train | 14-35 | | | | | | | 10 | L.H. | R. owens |
| " " | 14-35 | | | | | | | 11 | L. H. | " " |

Adviser or Director

Detailed records were kept to document the accomplishments of each flight student. In addition to academic grades, pilots received pink slips for any infractions of the rules. Three pink slips meant expulsion from the program. A check ride to ascertain proficiency in flight was one of the most dreaded experiences for cadets. (Private Collection.)

An instructor pilot gave a few words of advice to a fledgling pilot at Tuskegee Army Air Field. While the rate of elimination for cadets at Tuskegee was high, many of the men recalled that their instructors tried to help them make it through the training successfully. Only a few of the white instructors were routinely biased against the cadets. (Private Collection.)

Meteorologists played an important role in the safety of fliers. Inclement weather could prove deadly even for experienced pilots. Meteorology equipment included weather balloons, maps, barometers, and sextants. Sextants were used to determine position by the measurement of the angle between a heavenly body and the horizon or another star. (Private Collection.)

Personnel orders dated July 26, 1944, effective August 4, 1944, rated 23 single-engine combat pilots in Class 44-G as having completed pilot training. Eleven pilots were commissioned as second lieutenants, the remainder as flight officers. Maury Reid (second from right, middle row) was severely injured while test-flying a recently repaired aircraft just weeks after graduation and was forced to leave the Air Corps. (Private Collection.)

The daily flight board detailed each pilot's mission. Coordinates, landmarks, alternate fields, and reports of weather conditions were all necessary to ensure a pilot's safe return. Throughout a flight, pilots constantly searched for alternate landing fields for use in the event of an engine failure or other emergency. (Private Collection.)

Willis E. Sanderlin graduated in May 1945 at Tuskegee Army Air Field as a member of Class 45-C-SE. He served as a fighter pilot in the 99th Fighter Squadron and the 332nd Fighter Group. Sanderlin also flew as a bomber pilot with the 477th Composite Group at Lockbourne. (Private Collection.)

Henry C.L. Bohler spent several days eating high-calorie foods so as to meet the minimum weight requirement to pass his admission physical. He became a member of Class 44-J-SE at Tuskegee Army Air Field. Upon graduation as a fighter pilot in the 99th Fighter Squadron, he was assigned to Walterboro Army Air Field, and subsequently, Godman Field. (Private Collection.)

Students discussed possible problems with an instructor prior to a flight. Anticipating any and all possible difficulties such as engine malfunctions, bad weather, and inoperative radios better prepared the new pilots for actual in-flight emergencies. Spann Watson (far left) returned from combat in Europe to serve as an instructor pilot. (Private Collection.)

Each practice mission began with a briefing by instructors. Following graduation, pilots received combat readiness training at Walterboro Army Air Field, in Walterboro, South Carolina. African-American pilots stationed in Walterboro found that German prisoners of war received better treatment from the local population than they did. (Private Collection.)

This official photograph presented the perfect image of an Army Air Corps pilot. Theopolis W. Johnson was one of seven twin-engine pilots to graduate in Class 45-B-TE at Tuskegee Army Air Field. For Johnson, his fellow classmates, and all of the other members of the 477th Bombardment Group, the opportunity to serve overseas during World War II never came. Combat in Europe ended only weeks after his graduation; the war in the Pacific ended soon afterward. Following the deactivation of the bomber group, Johnson flew F-47s as a member of the 332nd Fighter Group. One of the Tuskegee Airmen who served in more than one war, Johnson was a member of the United States Air Force in Korea. (United States Air Force.)

# Three
# LIFE AT TUSKEGEE

The wooden barracks at Tuskegee Army Air Field were "home sweet home" for the duration of training for most of the men. Accommodations weren't luxurious, but they were better than those experienced by the early classes. The first class of 13 flight trainees had been housed on the campus of Tuskegee Institute. Their barracks was the old bathhouse at the renovated Phelps Hall. They took their meals in a private dining room at Tompkins Hall. Subsequent classes faced a different situation. Construction of Tuskegee Army Air Field began in June 1941. Roads and air fields had to be carved from the rural countryside. The former farmland was transformed into a small city. Administration buildings, a commissary, chapel, aircraft hangars, mess halls, classrooms, and housing sprang into existence within months. Prior to completion of the base, the trainees, along with numerous support personnel from Chanute Army Air Field, were housed in tents. By comparison, the barracks were a vast improvement. (Private Collection.)

Writing home provided an important emotional release for cadets, as well as a chance to relate experiences to friends and relatives. The moral support provided by friends and families was essential to the well-being of the men. Letters from home were read repeatedly and meant more to the men than gold. (Private Collection.)

The base library provided technical, as well as recreational, reading material. Many of the men possessed advanced degrees from some of the most prestigious black colleges across the nation. The entire football team from Morris Brown College applied for admission to the flight training program at Tuskegee Army Air Field. (Private Collection.)

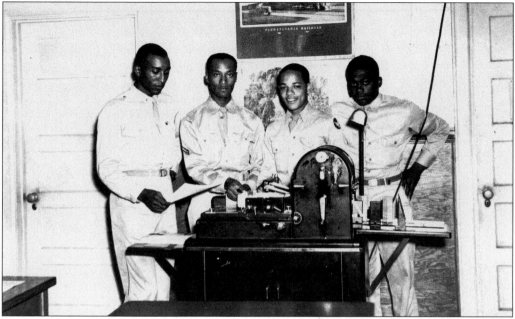

Base publications featured information on facilities, activities, and personnel at Tuskegee Army Air Field. Published by the cadets, the *Hawk's Cry* served as the base newspaper and contained news of the war, base gossip, sports scores, jokes, and coming attractions at the base theater. (Private Collection.)

The administration of a large Army Air Corps base was always difficult. The policies of segregation in both American military and civilian life made the job that much more difficult. Colonel Noel F. Parrish frequently flew to Washington to lobby the Air Corps on behalf of his men. Although a Southerner by birth, Parrish empathized with the difficulties faced by his men. (Private Collection.)

White-owned stores in Tuskegee, Alabama, did not welcome the African-Americans from Tuskegee Army Air Field. Fortunately, most necessities, including food, clothing, and cigarettes, were available from the base commissary. In most cases, the commissary offered a better selection of goods than the few stores in the black community. (Private Collection.)

Most cadets went into the town of Tuskegee infrequently, largely because of the hostile atmosphere which greeted them. From the beginning of the base construction, the local citizenry made their displeasure with the location of the air field known to all. Shopping at the base commissary made it possible for the men to avoid confrontations. (Private Collection.)

It has been said that an army travels on its stomach. This mess hall was recognized as providing the best meals at Tuskegee Army Air Field. Like most other facilities on the base, de facto segregation was the norm. Most white officers preferred not to eat their meals on the base. (Private Collection.)

While not necessarily considered gourmet dining, the meals provided by Tuskegee Army Air Field's dietitian, Mrs. Lillie S. Drew, were filling and nutritious. High in starches and carbohydrates, the meals provided cadets with energy for the vigorous activities of training. (Private Collection.)

Ceremonies were marked by a fanfare of trumpets. While visits by dignitaries happened periodically, one of the most important occasions was the graduation of the pilot training classes. Beginning with Class 42-C on March 6, 1942, graduations continued until Tuskegee Army Air Field closed after the war. The last class (46-C) graduated on June 28, 1946, although several more classes were still in training when the base closed a few months later. (Private Collection.)

The 313th Tuskegee Army Air Field band, under the direction of Captain Frank L. Drye, provided music for parades and ceremonies. A perennial favorite was the fight song of the 99th Fighter Squadron. Alvin J. Downing, a subsequent commander of the band at Tuskegee, later wrote the official song for Tuskegee Airmen, Inc. (Private Collection.)

Always exciting and spirited, athletic events at Tuskegee Army Air Field included field and track competitions. Many of the participants were top collegiate or semiprofessional athletes. Frequently part of a field day, activities would include tug-of-war competitions, piggy-back races, and dances. (Private Collection.)

Gunnery meets provided a chance to improve training skills as well as a recreational opportunity. Competition on the rifle range was every bit as intense as on any football field, track, or baseball diamond. Cadets had very little free time which wasn't filled with one form of activity or another. (Private Collection.)

In an area where segregation was the norm, residents of Tuskegee, Alabama, did not welcome the African-American airmen. For many of the white enlisted personnel at the base, the idea of black Army Air Corps officers had no appeal. In an effort to ensure their success in the training program and avoid potential conflict in town, many of the men never left the base. Attempting

to raise sagging morale at Tuskegee Army Air Field, Colonel Noel F. Parrish brought many well-known entertainers to the base. USO shows made frequent appearances. Ella Fitzgerald, Cab Calloway, and Count Basie were among the celebrities who performed for the troops. A special treat for the men was the appearance of legendary boxer Joe Louis. (Private Collection.)

Autographed photos ("pin-ups") of beautiful female entertainers such as Dodo Proctor and Coral Greer were cherished by many of the cadets. Lena Horne was one of the most famous and certainly one of the most beautiful entertainers to visit Tuskegee. She was everyone's favorite pin-up. (Private Collection.)

A highlight of Aviation Cadet Nasby Wynn's experience at Tuskegee Army Air Field was dancing with celebrity Lena Horne during one of her visits to the base. A tattered and torn photograph of their dance together remained a cherished possession years after the war ended. (Private Collection.)

46

*Roger* was hailed as one of the best all-soldier shows ever produced. Traveling throughout America for the Red Cross War Fund, the cast of 75 included the Glee Club, a number of specialty acts, the renowned TAAF Marching Band, and "The Imperial Wings of Rhythm." *Roger* was produced by the Tuskegee Army Air Field Personnel Services Department. (Private Collection.)

The theme of *Roger* focused on the supposed happenings at an army base when the scheduled all-star USO troupe failed to appear. The disappointed soldiers staged their own show, impersonating the famous Hollywood stars who had been slated to perform. Making fun of the glitches and "snafus" of military life was one way of relieving tension and raising the morale of the men at Tuskegee Army Air Field. (Private Collection.)

★ ★ ★ ★ ★ ★ ★ ★ ★ ★ ★ ★ ★ ★ ★ ★ ★ ★

TUSKEGEE ARMY AIR FIELD

PRESENTS

# ROGER

MUSICAL EXTRAVAGANZA

CITY AUDITORIUM
Birmingham, Ala.
Friday Evening 8:00 o'clock, June 29th

★ ★ ★ ★ ★ ★ ★ ★ ★ ★ ★ ★ ★ ★ ★ ★ ★

Tuskegee's swing band, "The Imperial Wings of Rhythm," included star musicians from some of the nation's top bands. Sergeant Claude Garvey, formerly of the "Savoy Sultans," was one of the musicians who, as did many of the men in the military, put a promising career on hold for the duration of the war. (Private Collection.)

Dancing to the music of "The Imperial Wings of Rhythm" was a pleasurable aspect of life at Tuskegee. Coeds from Tuskegee Institute, Spelman College, and other neighboring schools came to the base for dances and other special occasions. Many of the men met their future wives at these social events. (Private Collection.)

A Christmas Eve broadcast from Tuskegee featured carols sung by the cadets. Special holiday programs helped to ease the sadness caused by being separated from loved ones at Christmas. This loneliness would only get worse when the men were sent overseas. (Private Collection.)

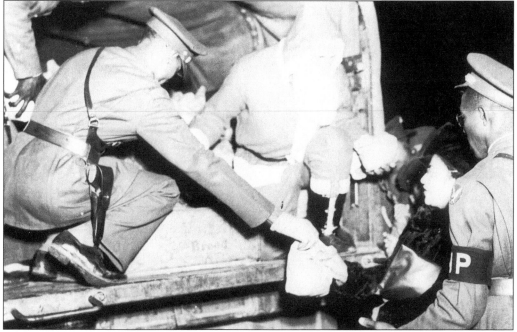

Even during wartime, Santa Claus managed to make a visit to Tuskegee Army Air Field. Each cadet's list was headed by a wish for a pair of shiny silver Air Corps wings. Festive holiday meals at the field's mess hall and packages and letters from families made Christmas away from home more bearable. (Private Collection.)

Tuskegee Army Air Field underwent rapid construction. One of the most easily-recognizable buildings was the post chapel. Following completion, it was the scene of weekly church services, weddings, and other religious celebrations. (Private Collection.)

Weddings were a special part of life at Tuskegee, especially around graduation week. Graduation Day, June 27, 1944, was the occasion for the double military wedding of Lieutenant and Mrs. Lewis Lynch and Lieutenant and Mrs. Hugh White. Both brides wore traditional wedding attire, although newspapers occasionally reported accounts of bridal gowns made from parachutes. (Private Collection.)

Most of the cadets were single during the training program. Nasby Wynn and Doris R. Lavarr were married on March 21, 1944, in the post chapel at Tuskegee Army Air Field. With graduation still several months in the future, leave was impossible, precluding an extended honeymoon. (Private Collection.)

While only a few of the cadets were married, some of the other personnel at the base had wives and families. The post chapel was also the scene of at least one baptism ceremony. For the officers and men who went overseas, it would be at least a year before they saw their families again. (Private Collection.)

Aviation Cadet Hiram E. Mann was one of the few married cadets in the Tuskegee Army Air Field flying program. Mann credited his wife, Kathadaza, for much of his success during the rigorous training at Tuskegee. While the Manns had experienced discrimination in the Midwest, neither was prepared for the blatant racism in the South. Accustomed to shopping in large department stores in Chicago, Mrs. Mann found that African-Americans were forbidden to try on clothing prior to purchase in Tuskegee. Employment of the same type as her former civil service position was unavailable. Military housing for families of the African-American cadets was also nonexistent, forcing her to rent a room from a family in the black community in Tuskegee. (Private Collection.)

Charles A. Hill Jr. and Mary Morgan both left their hometown of Detroit, Michigan, to enlist in the armed forces. Following graduation from Tuskegee Army Air Field in Class 44-F-SE, Lieutenant Charles Hill went to Europe as a single-engine fighter pilot, flying 28 combat missions. Captain Mary Morgan served at Camp Myles Standish and acted as the billeting officer for the Boston Port of Embarkation. Married following his return from Europe in October 1945, they were both assigned to Tuskegee Army Air Field, where he served as a base administrative officer, handling budget and fiscal matters. Reductions in flight time required all pilots to hold dual duty assignments. Mary Morgan Hill instructed the returning combat pilots in the handling of their newly assigned administrative duties. Both Charles and Mary Hill served at Tuskegee until the base's closing in September 1946. (Private Collection.)

Frederick D. Patterson and Colonel Benjamin O. Davis Jr. shared a quiet moment prior to the fourth anniversary celebration at Tuskegee Army Air Field. As president of Tuskegee Institute, Patterson had been one of the strongest advocates of the selection of Tuskegee for the location of the air field. Others had urged a less segregated area such as Chicago. (United States Air Force.)

Colonel Benjamin O. Davis Jr. addressed a large crowd on the fourth anniversary of the founding of Tuskegee Army Air Field. In his speech, Davis told the trainees how important it was for them to successfully complete the flight training program. While the individual men may not have felt that they were making history, Davis recognized the broader implications of the program's success. (Private Collection.)

*Four*

# FIGHTING THE
# ENEMY OVERSEAS

The original group of 99th Pursuit Squadron pilots, along with hundreds of support personnel, shipped out for Europe aboard the SS *Mariposa* on April 15, 1943. Landing in North Africa nine days later, the men were first stationed at Oued N'ja, near Fez. Lieutenant Philip Cochran, the Flip Corkin of the comic strip *Terry and the Pirates*, provided instruction in the P-40, labeling the men as natural-born dive bombers. Living conditions in North Africa mirrored those in the United States; the African-American airmen occupied one side of the base, white airmen the other. Segregation was still the norm, even in combat. A move to Fardjouna a month later gave the 99th its first taste of combat. As the only African-American members of the 33rd Fighter Group, they escorted bombers attacking Pantelleria, off the coast of Italy. For the men of the 99th Pursuit Squadron, later re-designated as the 99th Fighter Squadron, the war had begun. (Private Collection.)

Pilots from the 100th Fighter Squadron prepared for overseas deployment from Selfridge Field, Michigan, late in 1943. Following the formation of the 99th Fighter Squadron, pilots had continued to be trained at Tuskegee Army Air Field. The graduation of the successive pilot classes led to the activation of three additional squadrons—the 100th, 301st, and 302nd.

Eventually all four squadrons were sent into combat in Europe, where they comprised the 332nd Fighter Group. Although fighter groups traditionally were made up of only three squadrons, the all-black 332nd was an obvious exception. (Elwood T. Driver via National Air and Space Museum, Smithsonian Institution.)

During the days of a segregated air force, Colonel Benjamin O. Davis Jr., son of the Army's first African-American general, served as the commanding officer of the 99th Fighter Squadron, the 332nd Fighter Group, and eventually the 477th Composite Group. Colonel Davis went on to become the first African-American general in the United States Air Force. Few men, white or black, were more qualified to command troops than was Benjamin Davis. A staunch believer in education, physical fitness, and service to his country, Davis practiced what he preached. The first African-American to graduate in the 20th century from the United States Military Academy at West Point, Davis suffered four years of racial discrimination when his fellow West Point cadets refused to speak to him. Graduating 35th out of a class of 276 should have entitled him to the duty assignment of his choice. When he requested flight training, however, he was told that no black aviation units existed and his participation in a white unit would not be acceptable. The opening of the Army Air Corps to African-Americans in 1941 changed that. (Private Collection.)

Shortly after arriving in North Africa, in April 1943, the pilots of the 99th Fighter Squadron were supplied with Curtiss-Wright P-40 Warhawk airplanes. The Warhawk was armed with .50-caliber machine guns and was capable of carrying a 500-pound bomb. Many of the P-40s received by the 99th had previously seen service in various Allied air forces and were considered to be old and inferior. (Private Collection.)

Fighter pilots posed in front of a P-40. Powered by a 1,200-horsepower Allison engine, the P-40 had a cruising speed of approximately 300 miles per hour with a ceiling of 32,000 feet. While not the perfect airplane, the P-40 was attractive because it was available. Nearly 14,000 P-40s with various modifications were produced. (United States Air Force.)

On July 2, 1943, Charles B. Hall of Brazil, Indiana, earned the distinction of being the first African-American airman to shoot down an enemy aircraft. Shortly before 7 a.m., 12 silver P-40s took off on a mission to provide cover for a dozen North American B-25 bombers. The 99th Fighter Squadron had only one mission—protecting the slow-moving bombers as they headed to Sicily. Nearing the target, the Americans were attacked by almost a dozen Messerschmitt Me-109s and Focke-Wulf Fw-190s. Immediately the pilots of the 99th engaged the enemy in aerial combat. Flying his P-40 into the small aerial corridor between the bombers and the attacking Germans, Hall fired his machine guns at a Fw-190. Seconds later the German airplane spun out in flames. Returning to base, Hall received a royal reception. The men of the 99th celebrated a bittersweet victory; fellow pilots Sherman White and James McCullin had died in a midair collision. (National Air and Space Museum, Smithsonian Institution.)

Louis R. Purnell, Class 42-F-SE, was one of the original pilots in the 99th Fighter Squadron. Following his first tour of duty, Purnell was stationed at Tuskegee Army Air Field as an instructor pilot. Feeling that combat was safer, he returned to Europe for a second tour of overseas duty. A recipient of the Distinguished Flying Cross, Purnell flew 87 combat missions. (Private Collection.)

Enlisting in the Army Air Corps in November 1941, Spann Watson graduated at Tuskegee Army Air Field in Class 42-F-SE. As a member of the 99th Fighter Squadron and the 332nd Fighter Group, he flew 32 combat missions in Europe. Watson served as a combat readiness instructor at Walterboro Army Air Field following his return from Europe. (Private Collection.)

Among the African-American pilots, Lieutenant Lee A. Archer of the 332nd Fighter Group came the closest to being considered an "ace," with one probable and four definite German fighter planes to his credit. After filing into the briefing room at Ramitelli on October 12, 1944, 68 fighter pilots were briefed on the day's objective—an escort mission to Blechhammer, Germany. By the time the smoke of combat had cleared, the 332nd pilots had destroyed nine German fighters in the air. Flying his P-51 that day, Lee Archer had been responsible for destroying three. A graduate of Class 43-G-SE and a member of the 302nd Fighter Squadron, Archer was awarded the Distinguished Flying Cross and the Air Medal with 18 Oak Leaf Clusters for his service during World War II. As a jet pilot during the Korean Conflict, Archer commanded several fighter squadrons. (National Air and Space Museum, Smithsonian Institution.)

Andrew D. Turner was congratulated by a fellow pilot following a successful mission. A member of Class 42-I-SE and commanding officer of the 100th Fighter Squadron, Turner flew 69 combat missions. On a four-squadron mission on July 18, 1944, including pilots of the 99th, 100th, 301st, and 302nd Fighter Squadrons, the 332nd Fighter Group was assigned the job of providing coverage for the bombers of the 5th Bomb Wing against Memmingen Airdrome. In a dogfight with enemy fighters that lasted no more than a few minutes, several enemy aircraft were destroyed. Turner was credited with damaging one Messerschmitt Me-109; he received the Distinguished Flying Cross for his service in Europe. Under Colonel Benjamin O. Davis Jr., Turner became the deputy group commander of the 477th Composite Group in July 1945. While stationed at Lockbourne Army Air Base in Columbus, Ohio, Turner was killed in a midair collision on September 18, 1947. (Private Collection.)

Charles P. Bailey graduated as a single-engine pilot in Class 43-D-SE at Tuskegee Army Air Field. In *Josephine* and *My Buddy*, planes named after his parents, Bailey flew a total of 133 missions in the European-African Theater of Operations. For his combat accomplishments, he received the Air Medal with four Oak Leaf Clusters and the Distinguished Flying Cross. (Private Collection.)

Lieutenant Wendell C. Pruitt, a veteran of 70 combat missions, received congratulations from fellow pilot John F. Briggs. During the war in Europe, Pruitt was credited with downing three German fighters and sinking a Nazi destroyer escort. For these achievements, he received the Distinguished Flying Cross. Following his service in Europe, Pruitt was killed during a training mission while serving as a flight instructor at Tuskegee Army Air Field. (U.S. Air Force Photo Collection. Courtesy of National Air and Space Museum, Smithsonian Institution.)

Benjamin O. Davis Jr. served as the first commander of the 99th Fighter Squadron both at home and overseas. In September 1943, Davis returned to the United States, where he took command of the 332nd Fighter Group. By February 1944, Colonel Davis was back in Italy with the 332nd Fighter Group. Davis was frequently called upon to brief visiting dignitaries. (Private Collection.)

Few fathers could be more proud than General Benjamin O. Davis Sr. was as he presented the Distinguished Flying Cross to his son, Colonel Benjamin O. Davis Jr., in Italy on May 29, 1944. The only black general in the United States Army, General Benjamin O. Davis Sr. must have taken tremendous satisfaction in the accomplishments of the black Army Air Corps members. (U.S. Air Force Photo Collection. Courtesy of National Air and Space Museum, Smithsonian Institution.)

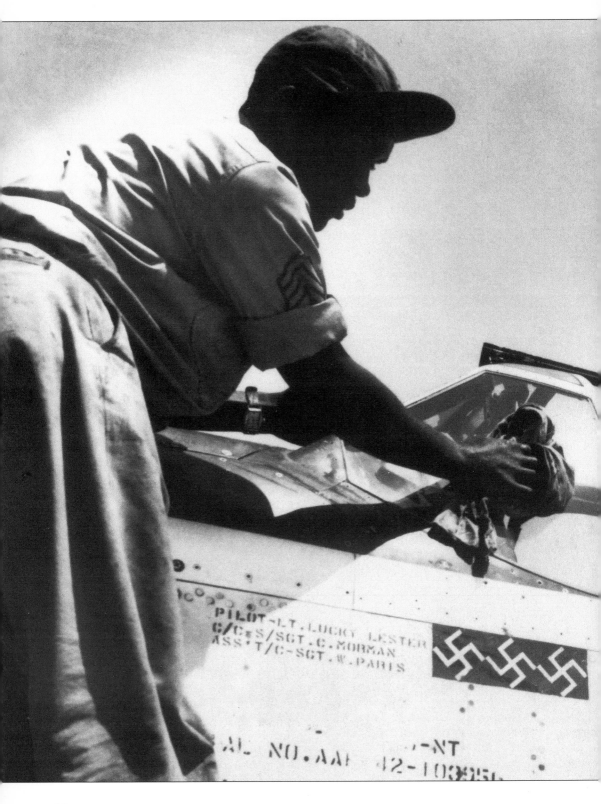

July 18, 1944, was a banner day for the pilots of the 332nd Fighter Group. As black P-51 Mustang pilots provided penetration coverage for American bombers of the 5th Bomb Wing against targets of opportunity in Memmingen, they were attacked by several large concentrations of enemy fighter planes. On a day in which several pilots of the 332nd Fighter Group flew back to base basking in the glory of victory, one in particular stood out. Clarence D. "Lucky" Lester scored three kills against deadly Messerschmitt Me-109s, considered by some aviation experts to be one of the finest single-seat fighter planes ever produced. On September 10, 1944, in an impressive ceremony, several pilots of the 332nd Fighter Group, including Clarence "Lucky" Lester, Joseph D. Elsberg, Jack Holsclaw, and Benjamin O. Davis Jr., were awarded the Distinguished Flying Cross. (U.S. Air Force Photo Collection, USAF Neg. No. 53700AC; courtesy of National Air and Space Museum, Smithsonian Institution.)

Colonel Benjamin O. Davis Jr. prepared to brief the Red Tail fighter pilots before a mission. On March 24, 1945, Colonel Benjamin O. Davis Jr. led the 332nd Fighter Group on one of the longest missions carried out by the 15th Air Force. While providing coverage for B-17 bombers on a 1,600-mile round-trip mission to Berlin, 59 P-51 Mustang pilots encountered more than 25 German defenders, many flying jet aircraft. The 332nd received the Distinguished Unit Citation for escorting the Allied bombers as they attacked the Daimler Benz Tank Works. (United States Air Force.)

During the first half of 1944, the 99th Fighter Squadron was headquartered at Capodichino Air Field, near Naples, Italy. One of their missions was to provide aerial support to Allied ship convoys. Flying their P-40s, the black pilots had frequent encounters with enemy Focke-Wulf and Messerschmitt aircraft. One of the most exciting days of the war for the 99th was January 27, 1944, when they were credited with the destruction of eight enemy airplanes. (Private Collection.)

The 332nd Fighter Group was assigned a strafing mission against ships, radio stations, and motor launches in the area of Trieste on June 25, 1944. While returning from their targets, eight 332nd P-47s crossing the Adriatic Sea came upon a German destroyer escort. A pair of P-47s made an initial pass against the ship, followed by an all-out assault by all eight American airplanes. The ship exploded and sank. (Private Collection.)

Few missions were more dangerous than low-level strafing. Captain Armour G. McDaniel nosed his P-51 toward an oil barge while firing his machine guns. As he pulled back on the control stick, the barge exploded, sending hundreds of pieces of jagged metal into his P-51. With difficulty, McDaniel returned to base, where he, his crew chief, and an armorer inspected the damage to his Mustang. (U.S. Air Force Photo Collection, USAF Neg. No. 56240AC; courtesy of National Air and Space Museum, Smithsonian Institution.)

Fighter pilots from the 332nd Fighter Group joined up in formation with other fighters of the 15th Air Force to provide escort for a flight of bombers to Germany. The hands-down favorite aircraft of the pilots, the P-51 Mustang was one of the finest American fighter planes produced for World War II. When the black squadrons received this airplane, they became a formidable opponent. African-American airmen destroyed 111 enemy aircraft in the air and damaged another 25. The red tails on the P-51s were a reassuring sight to Allied bomber crews. Renowned for staying with the bombers instead of abandoning them for targets of opportunity and greater glory, the Red Tails were frequently requested for escort duty. (U.S. Air Force Photo Collection, USAF Neg. No. 57476AC; courtesy of National Air and Space Museum, Smithsonian Institution.)

Previously assigned to the 12th Air Force, the 332nd Fighter Group was transferred to the 15th Air Force in May 1944. Their mission was to serve as bomber escorts on strategic bombing missions against targets in Central Europe. Less than a year later, the 332nd was credited with its 200th combat mission with the 15th Air Force without a loss. By February 1945, the African-American pilots had flown over 8,000 individual sorties. (Private Collection.)

Each day the Red Tails provided aerial protection for Allied bombers flying missions against Axis targets. This was one of the most important tasks of the black fighter pilots. Men of the 332nd Fighter Group posed next to a B-24 bomber decorated with artwork resembling Bugs Bunny. (National Air and Space Museum, Smithsonian Institution.)

This sign boasting a red-tailed P-51 Mustang leaves no doubt that this is headquarters of the 332nd Fighter Group. As the black squadrons transitioned out of P-40s and P-47s into the P-51 Mustangs, the tail assemblies of the aircraft they received were all in different paint schemes. Mechanics painted tails, trim tabs, and propeller spinners bright red. Black airmen quickly became known as the Red Tails. (Private Collection.)

As Allied forces recaptured enemy territory in Italy, the Air Corps bases advanced closer to their targets. Occasionally existing buildings could be adapted for military use. This headquarters building of the 332nd Fighter Group, for example, was an impressive structure. Most of the buildings on the base had a much less substantial appearance. (Private Collection.)

Military jeeps or army trucks were the usual modes of transportation at air bases in Italy. Most airmen lacked individual transportation. One enterprising member of the 332nd Fighter Group somehow managed to secure a motorcycle, an event which probably increased his popularity dramatically. (Private Collection.)

Constructing a base required men and materiel. When a camp had to be built, officers and enlisted men worked together. Frequently starting out as empty farmland, air bases materialized seemingly overnight. As enemy territory was recaptured and the front advanced, the bases were dismantled and relocated. (Private Collection.)

Winter rains turned the 332nd's camp into a mud pit, negating any images of warm and sunny Italy. Dry weather wasn't much of an improvement, however. When the fighters took off from the runways, clouds of dust obscured everything in sight. (Private Collection.)

Pets helped to bring a little civilization to camp life. The animals provided affection and companionship for homesick airmen. The men, in turn, shared their rations, substantially improving the diets of the hungry animals. (Private Collection.)

A typical base camp in Italy in 1945 wasn't very elegant. Protection from the elements was about the best that could be said for the accommodations. For young airmen far away from their loved ones, even a palace couldn't have compared favorably to home. (Private Collection.)

Any and all available materials were utilized to reinforce and winterize the military tents in which the men lived. Wooden packing cases became external walls, while other items were adapted to provide inside amenities. Make-shift camp stoves and aircraft fuel provided warmth against the winter chill. (Private Collection.)

The rugged individualism and self-confidence of pilots led to the personalization of "their" airplanes. What was painted on a pilot's airplane was defined only by his or his crew chief's imagination. Cartoon characters, beautiful women, and caricatures of Hitler and Mussolini all found a home on the nose of an airplane. Most fighter pilots, such as this one, opted for the name of a loved one. (Private Collection.)

Pilots often personalized their airplanes with names having special significance to them. Sometimes the names were of family members or loved ones back in America. Occasionally the names made a political statement. The meaning of this message is known only to the pilot. (Private Collection.)

Lieutenant Hiram E. Mann named his plane *Boss Lady*. *Duchess* recalled the nickname of Lieutenant Walter J. Palmer's wife. Lieutenant Robert W. Lawrence named his Mustang *Rick Lizzie* in honor of his wife. (Private Collection.)

The starboard side of Lieutenant Yenwith K. Whitney's P-51 Mustang bore the legend *Terry* in honor of his girlfriend. *Lovely Lady* was painted on the other side as a tribute to his mother. Whitney, a member of the 301st Fighter Squadron, flew 34 combat missions in Europe. (Private Collection.)

Each day as the black fighter pilots went into action, they had three hopes: staying alive, going home, and meeting up with an enemy fighter plane in the skies over Europe and Africa. Anyone lucky enough to engage the enemy and shoot him down had the right to have a swastika painted on the fuselage of his airplane. By the end of the war, 111 swastikas adorned the fuselages of airplanes flown by the African-American pilots. (Private Collection.)

The 332nd Fighter Group flew several missions on March 31, 1945. On a strafing mission near Linz, Austria, a flight of 17 Messerschmitts and Focke-Wulfs were engaged in combat. Pilots of the 332nd destroyed 13 enemy aircraft without a single loss to themselves. Lieutenant Bertram "Bert" Wilson, his crew chief, and an armorer proudly posed in front of *Skip's Wat*. That day Lieutenant Wilson had shot down a Focke-Wulf Fw-190. (Private Collection.)

The art work on a man's flight jacket was as individual as the personalized message on a pilot's airplane. This pilot chose to adorn the back of his jacket with the much venerated Red Tail P-51 Mustang, signifying that he was a member of the all-black 99th, 100th, 301st, or 302nd Fighter Squadrons. (Private Collection.)

Fighter pilots wore their squadron insignias with pride on their well-worn leather flight jackets. This pilot was a member of one of the African-American fighter squadrons, the 302nd. The insignia of the 302nd Fighter Squadron featured a winged red devil which was superimposed over a sky-blue disc. (Private Collection.)

Yenwith K. Whitney graduated as a member of Class 44-F-SE at Tuskegee Army Air Field. Returning after the war as an experienced combat fighter pilot, Whitney responded to advertisements seeking pilots for Eastern Airlines. With the hiring center located in Miami, Florida, it was quickly made clear that the positions were not available to African-Americans. (Private Collection.)

Commissioned at the age of 19, Harry T. Stewart Jr., Class 44-F-SE, flew 43 missions in Europe. He was credited with destroying three enemy aircraft in aerial combat. A pilot in the 332nd Fighter Group, Stewart was also a member of the winning team at the first United States Air Force Gunnery Meet at Las Vegas Air Force Base in 1949. (Private Collection.)

Charles Hill, a member of Class 44-F and combat pilot in Italy, shared a special bond with his crew chief. When Hill suffered a severe appendicitis attack during a mission, his crew chief put his own life in jeopardy. As the nearly unconscious Hill attempted to land his plane, quick action by tower personnel and his crew chief averted a crash and possibly saved Hill's life. (Private Collection.)

Hiram E. Mann graduated from Tuskegee Army Air Field on June 27, 1944 (Class 44-F-SE), as a single-engine combat fighter pilot. He served in the European-African Theater of Operations and flew 48 combat missions with the 302nd and later the 301st Fighter Squadron of the 332nd Fighter Group. (Private Collection.)

In the event of no scheduled missions or bad weather, many pilots donned dress uniforms and visited the officers' club. Flight suits served as the working attire for the airmen. The officers' club served several purposes; commander's calls, USO shows, and press briefings were frequently held in the club. (Private Collection.)

The officers' club for the 301st Fighter Squadron was perhaps not the most elegant of facilities on the base, but it was one of the most popular. After a mission, the officers' club was the perfect place to unwind, have a drink, and relive the day. (Private Collection.)

Pilots returning from combat missions were often greeted by Red Cross workers with hot coffee and doughnuts. The contributions of the Red Cross workers were greatly appreciated by the airmen and have received little recognition. (Private Collection.)

American airmen always befriended village children, frequently sharing candy and extra food with them. Black airmen received less racial discrimination from the European citizenry than from their fellow Americans. When asked why they were willing to fight for a nation that treated them so inequitably, the airmen inevitably responded that right or wrong, America was still their country. (Private Collection.)

The Air Corps-imposed quota system in the pilot training program resulted in a shortage of replacement pilots. This meant that the African-Americans flew many more missions than their white counterparts, who went home after 50 missions. Although the war in Europe had ended months earlier, most of the black personnel were not sent home until October 1945. While waiting to be sent home, many African-American airmen took an opportunity to see the sights in Italy. (Private Collection.)

Returning airmen relaxed aboard the SS *Woodbury* while en route to New York from Italy after the war. Filled with members of the 332nd Fighter Group, the Liberty ship resembled a floating military base. The *Woodbury Roller*, the ship's newspaper, chronicled the daily activities aboard the ship as well as news from America during the 17-day homeward journey. (Private Collection.)

Coming home at the end of the war in Europe was a joyous time for troops and families alike. The occasion also had moments of frustration and anger, however. Members of the 332nd Fighter Group, returning to the United States aboard the SS *Woodbury*, found that little had changed in their absence. At the foot of the gangplank, signs directed returning black and white airmen in separate directions. (Private Collection.)

Liberty ships carrying returning troops to America after the end of the war were met with a rousing welcome. When the African-Americans returned to their communities across the United States, however, there were no welcoming parades or official celebrations. There were also no jobs, even for experienced fighter pilots seeking employment in America's growing airline industry. (Private Collection.)

The Distinguished Flying Cross was awarded to 95 African-American pilots during World War II for extraordinary achievement or action in combat. Such achievements were not without casualties. Lieutenant Andrew D. Marshall was among the many African-American men wounded during combat. His airplane was destroyed by anti-aircraft fire. (National Air and Space Museum, Smithsonian Institution, SI Neg. No. 97-17479.)

Walter D. Westmoreland of Atlanta, Georgia, was a member of Class 43-G-SE. The nephew of NAACP Secretary Walter White, Westmoreland was killed when his P-51 went down over Hungary following a bomber escort mission to Blechhammer, Germany. Sixty-six African-American airmen lost their lives in Europe. (Private Collection.)

*Five*

# IT TOOK MORE
# THAN PILOTS

Prior to a mission, these armorers of the 332nd Fighter Group prepared to load an aircraft with .50-caliber ammunition. Approximately ten men and women were required to provide the necessary support to keep one pilot flying. During World War II, more than 10,000 African-American men and women served as support personnel for the Tuskegee Airmen. Years later Colonel Benjamin O. Davis Jr. was quoted as saying, ". . . They all knew their jobs and gave their best. When it was decided to integrate the services, I had no trouble finding jobs for the enlisted technicians and mechanics. I received more requests for them than I could supply." Working in different capacities at home and overseas, the contributions of many people were required. Crew chiefs, mechanics, technical inspectors, clerical workers, medical personnel, supply clerks, photographers, and cooks were all vital to the success of the mission. (U.S. Air Force Photo Collection, USAF Neg. No. B24123AC; courtesy of National Air and Space Museum, Smithsonian Institution.)

An armorer loaded a P-51 Mustang with bands of .50-caliber ammunition. Each day, in combat, 60 to 70 aircraft had to be readied for the day's missions. Thousands of rounds of ammunition had to be loaded; machine guns, cannons, bomb racks, and gun sights needed to be checked. (U.S. Air Force Photo Collection, USAF Neg. No. 53702AC; courtesy of National Air and Space Museum, Smithsonian Institution.)

Ground crews were vital to the success of the 99th Fighter Squadron and the 332nd Fighter Group. Armorers performed routine inspections of the weapons and bombs, just as the mechanics did with the airplanes. A typical fighter squadron required a complement of 15 armorers. Airmen underwent a 14-week course of training to prepare them as armorers. (U.S. Air Force Photo Collection, USAF Neg. No. 56239AC; courtesy of National Air and Space Museum, Smithsonian Institution.)

Enlisted men were the unheralded heroes of the war. This crew chief worked around the clock to have his pilot's airplane ready for action. Without the help of the ground crews, the pilots would never have flown, let alone been so successful. Tuskegee Airmen are not only the pilots, but also the vital support personnel. (Private Collection.)

A crew of several men was necessary to ensure that each fighter plane was ready to go. The crew chief treated the airplane as if it belonged to him. Inspections of damage to the aircraft from enemy fire followed each combat mission. (Private Collection.)

Understandably, pilots received most of the credit for wartime exploits, although support personnel were just as important. On March 23, 1945, mechanics of the 366th Service Squadron spent all night installing external fuel tanks that would allow long-range flights. The next day the 332nd Fighter Group made a 1,600-mile round-trip to Berlin against the Daimler Benz Tank Works, providing coverage for B-17 bombers. Because of the large external fuel tanks, when relief aircraft were late, the 332nd continued on to Berlin. Attacked by enemy

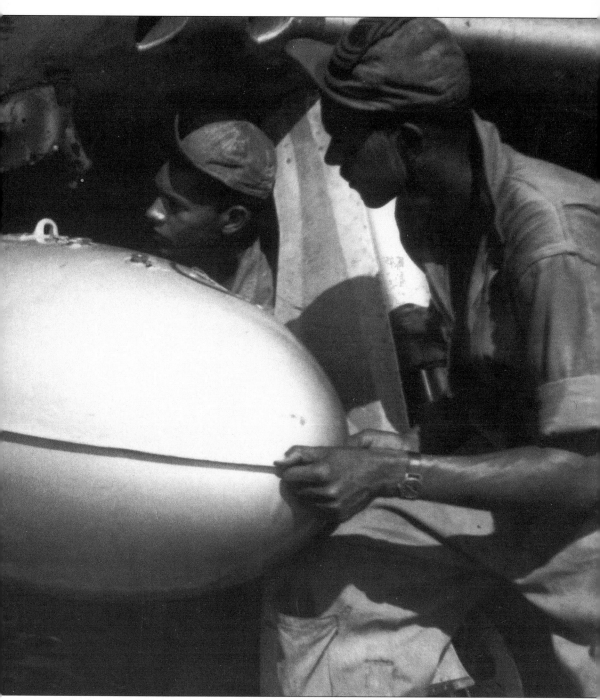

aircraft, the 332nd Fighter Group responded, destroying several German airplanes, including Messerschmitt Me-262 jets. For this mission, the 332nd Fighter Group was awarded the Distinguished Unit Citation, which read in part, ". . . ground crews worked tirelessly and with enthusiasm to have their aircraft at the peak of mechanical condition to insure the success of the operation." (U.S. Air Force Photo Collection, USAF Neg. No. 53697AC; courtesy of National Air and Space Museum, Smithsonian Institution.)

Safe airplanes were obviously as important as safe pilots. Mechanics performed line maintenance on a daily basis, as well as routine maintenance and major overhauls. In the early days of flight training at Tuskegee Institute, civilian mechanics, black and white, were hired to maintain the aircraft. When the 99th Pursuit Squadron was first activated at Chanute Field, Illinois, the table of organization called for the training of almost 200 mechanics. (Private Collection.)

Commanded by Captain Clarence F. Jones Jr., the members of the 889th Basic Flying Training Squadron made sure that the aircraft engines were in top condition. Even minor accidents required extensive repair and testing afterward to ensure the airworthiness of the planes. (Private Collection.)

Airplanes at Tuskegee were as thick as a swarm of mosquitoes on a hot summer night. There was the training of fighter, bomber, and liaison pilots. Each time an airplane flew, it had to be inspected and refueled. Mechanics spent many long and hot days in the Alabama sun laboring over an airplane to ensure the pilot's safety. (Private Collection.)

During the early days of pilot training at Tuskegee, aircraft maintenance was performed by a handful of civilians. At the same time, more than 150 enlisted men were being trained at Chanute Army Air Field as mechanics, welders, and metal workers. By war's end, the rolls of black Army Air Forces mechanics had grown exponentially. From that humble beginning in 1941, there were then nearly 2,000 aircraft mechanics. (Private Collection.)

Women played many vital roles at Tuskegee. These women were mechanics at Moton Field. After serving apprenticeships, several women became mechanics and line workers. They were responsible for providing maintenance, starting airplane engines, washing, and fueling aircraft. Carrie Campbell was a member of the base's guard staff and manned a post at the primary field's gate. Several wives of flight instructors served in clerical positions. (Private Collection.)

Support staff kept the planes flying. A sergeant made sure parachute rigging was secure. A well-made and carefully packed parachute provided a measure of safety for the aircraft pilots and crews in the event of an emergency. During World War I, American airmen were not issued parachutes. (Private Collection.)

Women were important to the mission. Alice Dungey Gray's domain was the 14-by 19-foot parachute-riggers' workroom. The one-time Louisiana schoolteacher was in charge of the parachute rigging department. Mildred Hanson, a graduate of Tuskegee Institute's first Civilian Pilot Training Program class and holder of a private pilot's license, was also licensed by the Civil Aeronautics Authority as a parachute rigger and worked with Gray. (Private Collection.)

Men from the 1451st Quartermaster Company made sure that troops had all of the necessities of life. The procurement and storage of supplies of clothing, food, and the thousands of other incidentals of military life were the responsibility of the Quartermaster Company. (Private Collection.)

Duties of the 964th Quartermaster Platoon included regular maintenance on the military vehicles at the base. Jeeps, trucks, and other military vehicles received heavy use and required constant care to ensure that they remained in smooth working condition. (Private Collection.)

In mid-September 1941, six medical officers reported for duty at Tuskegee. The following April female nurses arrived from Ft. Bragg. Major DeHaven Hinkson headed the team of doctors, dentists, nurses, technicians, and aides staffing a 25-bed hospital complete with operating room. First Lieutenant Della Raney, the first African-American nurse to report for duty during World War II, was Tuskegee Army Air Field's chief nurse. (Private Collection.)

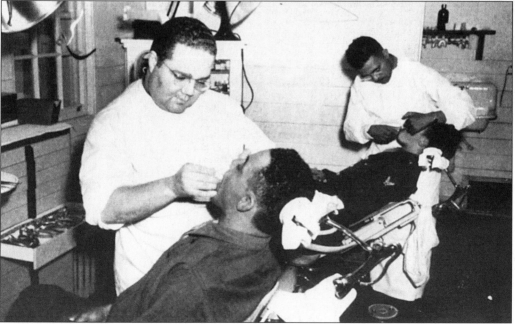

A toothache can be a minor inconvenience or a major pain. To alleviate potential problems, especially while overseas, dental care was an important part of the preparation for military life at Tuskegee Army Air Field. (Private Collection.)

Especially in the days before computers, any large bureaucracy generated huge quantities of paper work. The Army Air Corps was certainly no exception. While the captains, majors, and colonels were credited with the smooth running of the bases, unheralded office clerks and noncommissioned officers were frequently the ones who really maintained the organization. (Private Collection.)

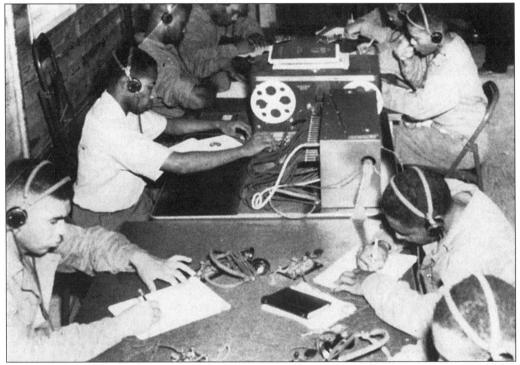

Dots and dashes, or short and long signals, were sent when a key or lever opened and closed an electrical circuit. The transmission of coded messages in this manner was known as telegraphy and was one of the duties performed by members of the Communications Company. Switchboard and radio communications were also part of their area of expertise. (Private Collection.)

Donald A. Williams served at Tuskegee Army Air Field and Malden Army Air Field before being transferred to overseas duty in the Philippines. A statistical draftsman, he charted the progress made by cadets in the training programs. Like many African-Americans, Williams conducted his own personal battles against segregation at each base where he was stationed. (Private Collection.)

A firm of black architects, McKissack and McKissack, designed Tuskegee Army Air Field, which then grew by leaps and bounds. It was up to the base drafting department to develop the plans for expansion and to compile statistical information on the program. (Private Collection.)

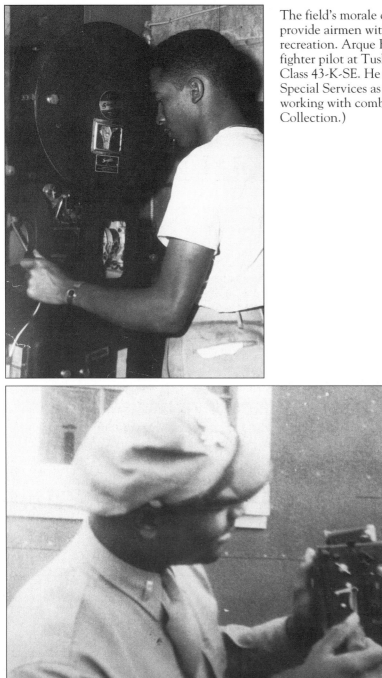

The field's morale officer did his best to provide airmen with movies for off-duty recreation. Arque B. Dickerson trained as a fighter pilot at Tuskegee Army Air Field in Class 43-K-SE. He also served in the Special Services as a technical instructor, working with combat veterans. (Private Collection.)

Before the invention of modern disposable cameras, the base photographer documented aspects of military life. Upon graduation from Officer Candidate School, Alvin J. Downing was assigned to the Special Services unit, and later directed the 313th Army Air Forces Band at Tuskegee Army Air Field. (Private Collection.)

# Six

# FIRST FIGHTERS, THEN BOMBERS

The United States War Department and the generals who led the Army Air Corps had no more interest in African-Americans becoming bomber pilots than they had in blacks flying single-engine airplanes. As was the case with the 99th Fighter Squadron, pressure from black civic, business, and political leaders led to the formation of the all-black bomber squadrons. Activated at Selfridge Field, Michigan, in 1943, the 477th Bombardment Group (Medium) was composed of the 616th, 617th, 618th, and 619th Bombardment Squadrons. The newly formed 477th was supposed to have a complement of 1,200 officers and men. Sixty B-25 twin-engine Mitchell bombers, each capable of carrying a bomb load of 2,000 pounds, would perform the medium-range bombing mission of the 477th. With 60 B-25 bombers costing $125,000 each and estimated officer training costs of $35,000 each, the initial cost of activating the 477th Bombardment Group was estimated at 20 million dollars. (Private Collection.)

Pilots from Class 44-H-TE listened as Captain James G. White, their squadron commanding officer, provided a briefing on a cross-country flight at Douglas Army Air Field in Arizona. Basic and Advanced Flying School curriculums included classes in cross-country flight. (United States Air Force.)

Bomber pilots of Class 44-J-TE posed for a class photograph for posterity. Following pilot training at Tuskegee Army Air Field, bomber crews attended B-25 transition school at Mather Field in California. Mather Field was an integrated base until a visiting general complained and caused mess facilities to be segregated. Black officers refused to eat at a segregated mess and paid to eat their meals at the base's integrated post exchange. (Private Collection.)

In 1939, less than 200 African-Americans were licensed to fly an airplane. That would soon change. The first class of single-engine fighter pilots graduated from Tuskegee on March 7, 1942. Twin-engine bomber pilots soon followed, with that first class graduating on December 5, 1943. By war's end, nearly 1,000 young black men had graduated from Tuskegee's flying school. (Private Collection.)

The pilots and crews of the 477th Bombardment Group were destined never to go overseas during World War II. Instead they remained on their home soil and fought many organized and personal battles against segregation and racism from Army Air Corps leaders. The bomber crews never received the medals and commendations as did their counterparts in the fighter squadrons. However, the battles they fought were just as important. (Private Collection.)

The home base of the 477th Bombardment Group was Selfridge Field, Michigan. The role of the 477th was to fly B-25 twin-engine Mitchell bombers. The North American B-25 was designed prior to World War II. With a length of 53 feet and a wingspan of approximately 68 feet, the B-25 had a cruising speed of 250 miles per hour. More than 10,000 North American B-25s were constructed. A flight of B-25s, which took off from a carrier deck and were led by Jimmy Doolittle, made the historic attack on Tokyo in April 1942. Training for this flight had taken place in secret at Eglin Field, Florida. Many black fighter pilots had honed their aerial gunnery skills at the same field. The reception they received there was far less hospitable than that accorded Doolittle's Raiders. (Private Collection.)

Eliminated from pilot training because of color blindness, Jean R. Esquerre served as a radio operator/gunner on B-25 aircraft with the 477th Bombardment Group. A B-25 flight crew included pilots, navigators, bombardiers, gunners, radio operators, and ground crew. (Private Collection.)

Activation of the 477th Bombardment Group required the training of not only pilots, but also navigators and bombardiers. The initial training of African-American bomber pilots was at Tuskegee. Gunners learned their craft at Eglin Field, Florida; navigators and bombardiers were trained at fields in Texas. (Private Collection.)

Six members of a B-25 flight crew posed for a photograph at Godman Field in 1945. From left to right, they are as follows: (kneeling) Albert New, radio operator and waist gunner; Leroy Jackson, tail gunner; and Thomas Simon, engineer and top turret gunner; (standing) George Harbert, navigator and nose gunner; Nasby Wynn, pilot; and Henri Fletcher, pilot. (Private Collection.)

At Godman Field in Kentucky, maintenance crews made up of mechanics, welders, painters, and hydraulic and sheet metal specialists made sure that the 477th's B-25 bombers were always ready to fly. Painters took special delight in emblazoning the bomber stabilizers with unit designations. (Private Collection.)

Upon graduation, cadets were awarded their silver Air Corps wings and commissioned as either flight officers or second lieutenants. Showing great joy in the achievements of their sons, family members proudly assisted in the ceremonial pinning of the new pilot's wings. (Private Collection.)

Squadron A of the 118th Army Air Forces Base Unit assembled for review on a clear Kentucky morning at Godman Field. Captain Elizabeth C. Hampton was the commanding officer of the nearly 100 women who served in the WAC squadron. Second Lieutenant Margaret G. Allen acted as the squadron adjutant. (Private Collection.)

Pilots James A. Hurd and Augustus G. Brown of the 477th Bombardment Group looked to the future of an integrated Air Corps. Such a time had not yet arrived, however, in April 1945. Colonel Robert Selway, the white commander of the 477th, was an avowed segregationist who persisted in policies of discrimination, despite regulations to the contrary. When the black officers attempted to enter an illegally segregated officers' club at Freeman Field, more than 100 African-American officers were arrested. Although charges against most of the men were later dismissed, three officers underwent court-martial proceedings. A reversal in 1995 of the sole conviction finally ended this travesty of justice and brought an end to the Freeman Field Mutiny. (Private Collection.)

The chow line at Godman Field seemed to extend for miles. Hoping that the food would be worth the wait, hungry personnel lined up for meals at the base mess hall. Mess Sergeant Bell supervised the preparation of thousands of meals each week. (Private Collection.)

Many of the wooden buildings at Godman Field featured a board and batten style of construction. These barracks were located at the corner of Tenth Street and Second Avenue. The local white population was no more welcoming of the black airmen than they had been at Tuskegee, Chanute, or Selfridge Fields. (Private Collection.)

110

After serving two tours of duty in Europe during World War II, Colonel Benjamin O. Davis Jr. returned to the United States in April 1945. Colonel Robert Selway, one of the most despised officers the black airmen had ever known, was relieved of duty as commander of the 477th Bombardment Group in June 1945. With obvious irony, Colonel Benjamin O. Davis Jr. became the group's new commander on July 1, 1945. (Private Collection.)

This brick building presented a more substantial appearance than that of the many frame structures on the base. It served as the base headquarters for the 477th Composite Group at Godman Field, located 30 miles south of Louisville and adjacent to Fort Knox, Kentucky. (Private Collection.)

Lieutenant John Silvera briefed Colonel Benjamin O. Davis Jr. on the positive publicity achieved by the Tuskegee Airmen. So strong a hold did Davis have over the men in his command that some derisively referred to it as Ben Davis' Air Force. Others meant it as a compliment. (Private Collection.)

In early March 1946, Brigadier General Edward J. Timberlake, adjutant for the Army Air Forces Continental Command, announced that the 477th would be transferred to Lockbourne Army Air Base, located near Columbus, Ohio. Commanded by Colonel Benjamin O. Davis Jr., the 477th Composite Group consisted of two medium-sized bomber squadrons and the 99th and 100th Fighter Squadrons. For the first time, African-Americans commanded an Army Air Forces base without the immediate supervision of whites. (United States Air Force.)

In 1945, Major Vance H. Marchbanks Jr., the base flight surgeon at Godman Field, was awarded the Bronze Star by Colonel Benjamin O. Davis Jr. Marchbanks, a former member of the 332nd Fighter Group, later served as a member of the medical team that supported John Glenn's historic space flight as the first American to orbit the Earth in 1962. (Private Collection.)

Prior to the formation of the bomber squadrons, the Air Corps issued a report stating that "It is common knowledge that the colored race does not have the technical nor the flying background for the creation of a bombardment-type unit." Members of the 477th Bombardment Group proved the Air Corps wrong. Daniel "Chappie" James Jr. (center) went on to become the first African-American four-star general in the United States Air Force. (United States Air Force.)

The United States in the 1940s was deeply divided along racial lines in both the civilian and military populations. Although more overt in the South, segregation and discrimination existed everywhere. Many of the nation's military leaders, including Secretary of War Henry Stimson, General Frank O. Hunter, Colonel Frederick von Kimble, Colonel Robert Selway, and others, strongly believed in segregation. Transferred from base to base in an effort to derail their training and destroy morale, the members of the 477th Bombardment Group endured even greater racial discrimination than did the fighter squadrons. Shown climbing into his airplane, Nasby Wynn Jr. trained as a bomber pilot in Class 44-J-TE at Tuskegee Army Air Field. Following graduation, he served at a number of military locations with the 477th Bombardment Group, including Selfridge Field, Freeman Field, and Walterboro Army Air Field. (Private Collection.)

*Seven*

# AFRICAN-AMERICANS IN KOREA AND VIETNAM

The successes of the African-Americans in the Army Air Corps during World War II were at least in part responsible for the decision of President Harry Truman to integrate the United States military in 1948. Members of the Fahy Committee witnessed the signing by President Truman of Executive Order 9981 on July 26, 1948. The order proclaimed: "Whereas it is essential that there be maintained in the armed services of the United States the highest standards of democracy, with equality of treatment and opportunity for all who serve in our country's defense." With Truman's order, segregation in America's military was officially ended, but that was not always the reality. The Korean Conflict became a practical means to insure the integration of the armed forces, as African-Americans were received equally as American soldiers and airmen. If Korea was the initial means of military integration, Vietnam provided near-equality of opportunity in the air and on the battlefields of Southeast Asia. (U.S. Air Force Photo Collection; courtesy of National Air and Space Museum, Smithsonian Institution.)

The first United States Air Force Fighter Gunnery Meet, held at Las Vegas Air Force Base in May 1949, was won by the men of the 332nd Fighter Group. Upon their return, *The Lantern*, Lockbourne Air Force Base's newspaper, featured the victories of the 332nd Fighter Group as front-page news. Several months later, during deactivation of the 332nd, the top team trophy disappeared. Adding insult to injury, official Air Force records for years afterward made no mention of this victory. (United States Air Force.)

Accurate marksmanship resulted in the first-place victory of the 332nd Fighter Group at the initial United States Air Force Fighter Gunnery Meet in 1949. Alva N. Temple, Harry T. Stewart, James H. Harvey, and Halbert Alexander flew nearly obsolete F-47 propeller-driven airplanes against competition that flew F-80 and F-84 jets. Contests included aerial gunnery, panel gunnery, dive-bombing, skip-bombing, and rocketry. (United States Air Force.)

Lieutenant William E. Brown Jr. climbed into his North American F-86 Sabre prior to a mission in Korea in March 1953. Brown logged over 100 combat missions in the Korean Conflict and the same number in Southeast Asia during the Vietnam War. He eventually reached the rank of major general in the United States Air Force. (U.S. Air Force Photo Collection, USAF Neg. No. 116986AC; courtesy of National Air and Space Museum, Smithsonian Institution.)

Integration of the military meant that all-black units such as the 332nd Fighter Group and the 477th Bombardment Group no longer existed. An integrated Air Force B-26 crew flew the last combat mission of the Korean Conflict in July 1953. From left to right are Airman Third Class Dennis Judd, Lieutenant Donald Mansfield, and Lieutenant Bill Ralston. (U.S. Air Force Photo Collection; courtesy of National Air and Space Museum, Smithsonian Institution.)

Pilots of the 34th Tactical Group stationed at Qui Nhon, Republic of South Vietnam, prepared for a Douglas A1-E Skyraider strike against the enemy. From left to right are Captain James T. Harwood, First Lieutenant James H. Manly, and Captain Robert H. Tice. (National Air and Space Museum, Smithsonian Institution.)

Daniel "Chappie" James Jr. of Pensacola, Florida, was described as "a pilot's pilot." A member of the 477th Bombardment Group during World War II, James flew more than 100 combat missions in Korea and another 78 in Southeast Asia. He believed that one should "prove to the world that you can compete on an equal basis." (National Air and Space Museum, Smithsonian Institution.)

The wars in Korea and Vietnam were the first military actions in which blacks and whites truly served and died together. Hostile situations did not distinguish between races. Colonel Fred V. Cherry, an Air Force pilot, was held as a prisoner of war in North Vietnam for more than seven years. (National Air and Space Museum, Smithsonian Institution, SI Neg. No. 93-16145.)

Daniel "Chappie" James Jr. discussed military matters with President Lyndon B. Johnson. Commissioned a second lieutenant in July 1943, James became the first African-American to be promoted to four-star general in the United States Air Force. James served many command roles including deputy assistant secretary of defense, vice commander of the Military Airlift Command, and commander in chief of NORAD/ADCOM. (National Air and Space Museum, Smithsonian Institution, SI Neg. No. 178134USAF.)

Daniel "Chappie" James Jr., a former civilian instructor pilot at Tuskegee's Moton Field, graduated in Class 43-G at Tuskegee Army Air Field. In his early days as a student, James was expelled from Tuskegee Institute for fighting. During his illustrious military career, however, General James went on to become an excellent example for young men and women of all races. (National Air and Space Museum, Smithsonian Institution.)

While serving as president of Tuskegee Airmen, Inc., Jean Esquerre presented President Ronald Reagan with a Tuskegee Airman leather flying jacket. Formal acknowledgment of the accomplishments of the African-Americans who served in the Army Air Corps was lacking for many years. Only recently have their achievements received deserved recognition. (Private Collection.)

In 1974, Captain Lloyd "Fig" Newton was the first African-American pilot to become a member of the Thunderbirds, the Air Force demonstration squadron. During the war in Vietnam, Newton flew 269 combat missions in Southeast Asia. In March 1997, General Newton became commander of Air Education and Training Command. (National Air and Space Museum, Smithsonian Institution.)

Donnie L. Cochran was the first African-American to be selected as a member of the United States Navy Flight Demonstration Squadron. Cochran assumed command of the Blue Angels precision flight team in 1994. During his career in the United States Navy, Captain Cochran accumulated more than 5,350 flight hours, including 888 carrier landings. (Private Collection.)

Charles E. McGee was commissioned as a second lieutenant at Tuskegee Army Air Field on June 30, 1943. Flying P-39s, P-40s, and P-51s, he served as a combat pilot with the 302nd Fighter Squadron during World War II. McGee also flew P-51s during the Korean Conflict while serving with the 67th Fighter Bomber Squadron. Commander of the 16th Tactical Reconnaissance Squadron, he flew the RF-4C in Southeast Asia. For his military service, Colonel McGee has been awarded the Legion of Merit with an Oak Leaf Cluster, the Distinguished Flying Cross with two Oak Leaf Clusters, the Bronze Star, the Air Medal with 25 Oak Leaf Clusters, and numerous other decorations. He has served on two separate occasions as president of Tuskegee Airmen, Inc. (Private Collection.)

*Eight*

# BEYOND THE
# BOUNDARIES

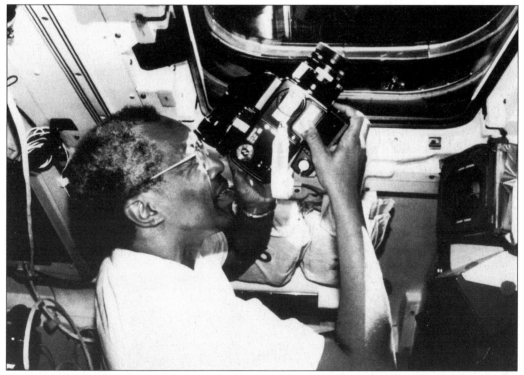

America's first manned space flight took place on May 5, 1961. It would not be for another 22 years that an African-American would fly in space. Just as African-Americans fought to serve their country as members of the Army Air Corps during World War II, they sought the opportunity to fly in the space program of the United States. As a *Challenger* crew member in August 1983, Guion S. Bluford became the first African-American to fly in space. Prior to entering NASA's training program in 1979, he served as a pilot in the United States Air Force, flying 144 combat missions in Southeast Asia. On board STS-53 *Discovery*, Bluford used a hand-held Hasselblad camera to photograph the Earth while on an eight-day mission in Earth orbit in 1992. During his career as an astronaut, Bluford had more than 650 cumulative hours of space flight. (National Aeronautics and Space Administration.)

Charles F. Bolden Jr. flew over 100 missions in Southeast Asia as an A6-A Intruder pilot. A veteran of three space flights, Bolden served as pilot on STS-61C *Columbia* in 1986 and STS-31 *Discovery* in 1990. In 1992, as mission commander on STS-45 *Atlantis*, Bolden commanded a crew of seven. This mission was significant in that it was the first Spacelab mission dedicated to NASA's Mission to Planet Earth. Bolden attained the rank of general in the United States Marine Corps. (National Aeronautics and Space Administration.)

As a crew member of the space shuttle *Challenger*, Dr. Ronald E. McNair tragically lost his life on January 28, 1986. His mission on the ill-fated flight would have been to deploy the Spartan-Halley satellite to track Halley's Comet. With a doctorate in physics from Massachusetts Institute of Technology, he worked as a laser physicist for Hughes Research Laboratories before joining NASA. On an earlier *Challenger* mission, Dr. McNair became the second African-American to orbit the earth. (National Aeronautics and Space Administration.)

In 1987, Dr. Mae C. Jemison became the first African-American woman to join the National Aeronautics and Space Administration as an astronaut. In her academic career, she earned undergraduate degrees in chemical engineering and African-American studies and a doctorate in medicine. Jemison worked with the Peace Corps in West Africa before entering the space program. As a mission specialist, Jemison conducted a joint Japanese-American life sciences project aboard the shuttle *Endeavour*. (National Aeronautics and Space Administration.)

Dr. Mae C. Jemison performed frog embryology experiments in a general purpose work station in the Spacelab-J module at NASA's Marshall Space Flight Center in Huntsville, Alabama, in 1992. The work was part of the preparation for a scheduled flight as a mission specialist on the STS-47 space shuttle. (National Aeronautics and Space Administration.)

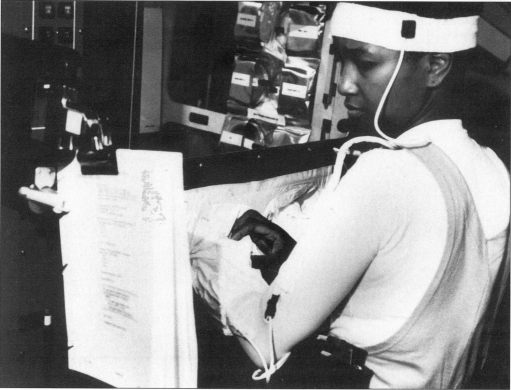

Dr. Bernard A. Harris Jr. joined NASA as a clinical scientist and flight surgeon in 1987. Following his selection in 1990 and becoming an astronaut in 1991, Harris made several flights into space. From February 2 through 11, 1995, Bernard Harris served as payload commander on STS-63, the first flight of the joint Russian-American space program. During this flight, Dr. Harris became the first African-American to walk in space. (National Aeronautics and Space Administration.)

Astronaut Frederick D. Gregory, a graduate of the United States Air Force Academy, served as a helicopter rescue pilot in Vietnam and later as a NASA test pilot. Gregory piloted the Orbiter *Challenger*, launched from Kennedy Space Center on April 29, 1985. In 1989, he served as spacecraft commander on *Discovery*. Gregory commanded a crew of six onboard the shuttle *Atlantis* as it orbited the earth 110 times in December 1991. Gregory was designated as an "Ira Eaker Fellow" by the Air Force Association. (National Aeronautics and Space Administration.)

Winston E. Scott accumulated more than 3,000 hours of flight time in 20 different military and civilian aircraft during his naval career. Selected as an astronaut in March 1992, he served as a mission specialist on STS-72. During the nine-day flight, the *Endeavour* crew tested techniques to be used in the assembly of the international space station. In his first space flight, Scott traveled almost 4 million miles and completed a space walk of 6 hours and 53 minutes. (National Aeronautics and Space Administration.)

Robert L. Curbeam Jr., a graduate of the United States Naval Academy, served as a naval aviator with aircraft carrier experience on board the USS *Forrestal.* As a member of Fighter Squadron 11, Curbeam was deployed to the Mediterranean and Caribbean Seas and the Arctic and Indian Oceans. Curbeam entered astronaut training in 1995. His first flight as an astronaut was as a mission specialist on STS-85 *Discovery,* where he logged over 284 hours in space. (National Aeronautics and Space Administration.)

Photographed by the crew of Apollo 17 en route to the moon, this spectacular view of the Earth extends from the Mediterranean Sea to Antarctica. The men and women of the Tuskegee Experience opened many doors for future aviators. African-Americans serving in the nation's military in Korea and Southeast Asia further helped to pave the way. As with the fighter squadrons of World War II, the efforts of many people are required to keep America's space program in operation. Approximately 1,000 technical, scientific, and engineering support personnel are needed to support each astronaut. Many of these men and women are African-Americans. Guion Bluford, Frederick Gregory, Bernard Harris, Winston Scott, Robert Curbeam, Ronald McNair, Mae Jemison, and the many other African-American members of America's space program have gone beyond the boundaries to reach for the stars. (National Aeronautics and Space Administration.)

128